452 total dots

⚠ = Begin a new line section.

◉ = Pick up your pen/pencil and look for the next sequential
number with the small triangle symbol next to it.

351 total dots

△ = Begin a new line section.

⊙ = Pick up your pen/pencil and look for the next sequential
number with the small triangle symbol next to it.

430 total dots

△ = Begin a new line section.

◉ = Pick up your pen/pencil and look for the next sequential
number with the small triangle symbol next to it.

451 total dots

⚠ = Begin a new line section.

◉ = Pick up your pen/pencil and look for the next sequential
   number with the small triangle symbol next to it.

380 total dots

⚠ = Begin a new line section.

◉ = Pick up your pen/pencil and look for the next sequential
number with the small triangle symbol next to it.

471 total dots

△ = Begin a new line section.

◉ = Pick up your pen/pencil and look for the next sequential
number with the small triangle symbol next to it.

418 total dots

△ = Begin a new line section.

◉ = Pick up your pen/pencil and look for the next sequential
number with the small triangle symbol next to it.

394 total dots

⚠ = Begin a new line section.

◉ = Pick up your pen/pencil and look for the next sequential
number with the small triangle symbol next to it.

352 total dots

⚠ = Begin a new line section.

◉ = Pick up your pen/pencil and look for the next sequential
number with the small triangle symbol next to it.

654 total dots

△ = Begin a new line section.

⊙ = Pick up your pen/pencil and look for the next sequential
number with the small triangle symbol next to it.

743 total dots

$\triangle$ = Begin a new line section.

$\odot$ = Pick up your pen/pencil and look for the next sequential
number with the small triangle symbol next to it.

527 total dots

⚠ = Begin a new line section.

◉ = Pick up your pen/pencil and look for the next sequential
   number with the small triangle symbol next to it.

390 total dots

⚠ = Begin a new line section.

⊙ = Pick up your pen/pencil and look for the next sequential
    number with the small triangle symbol next to it.

300 total dots

⚠ = Begin a new line section.

◉ = Pick up your pen/pencil and look for the next sequential
number with the small triangle symbol next to it.

666 total dots

△ = Begin a new line section.

⊙ = Pick up your pen/pencil and look for the next sequential
number with the small triangle symbol next to it.

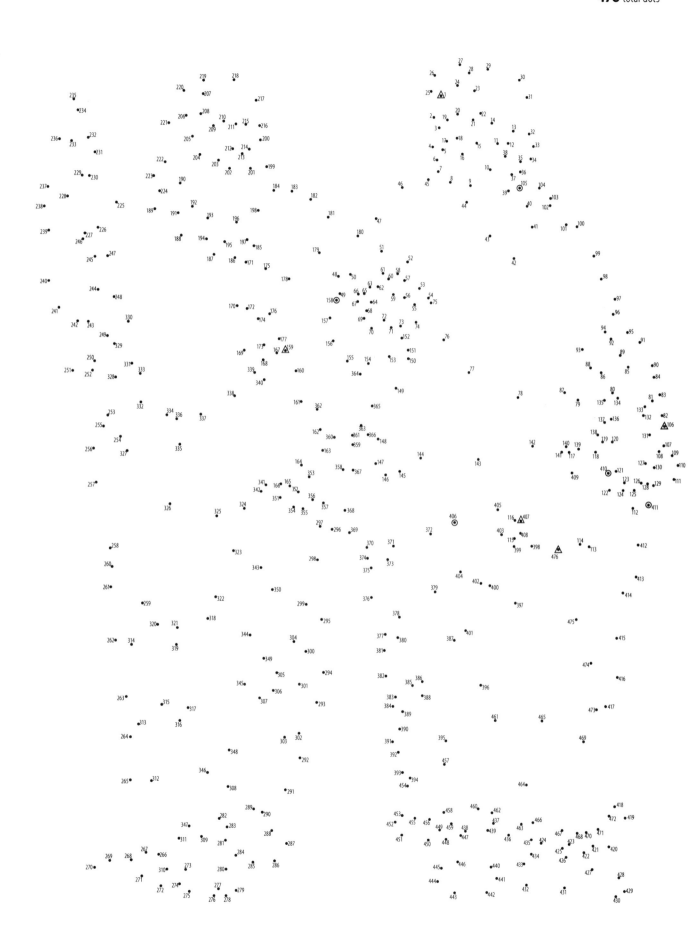

$\triangle$ = Begin a new line section.

$\odot$ = Pick up your pen/pencil and look for the next sequential
    number with the small triangle symbol next to it.

444 total dots

⚠ = Begin a new line section.

◉ = Pick up your pen/pencil and look for the next sequential
number with the small triangle symbol next to it.

730 total dots

⚠ = Begin a new line section.

◉ = Pick up your pen/pencil and look for the next sequential
number with the small triangle symbol next to it.

△ = Begin a new line section.

⊙ = Pick up your pen/pencil and look for the next sequential
number with the small triangle symbol next to it.

397 total dots

△ = Begin a new line section.

⊙ = Pick up your pen/pencil and look for the next sequential
number with the small triangle symbol next to it.

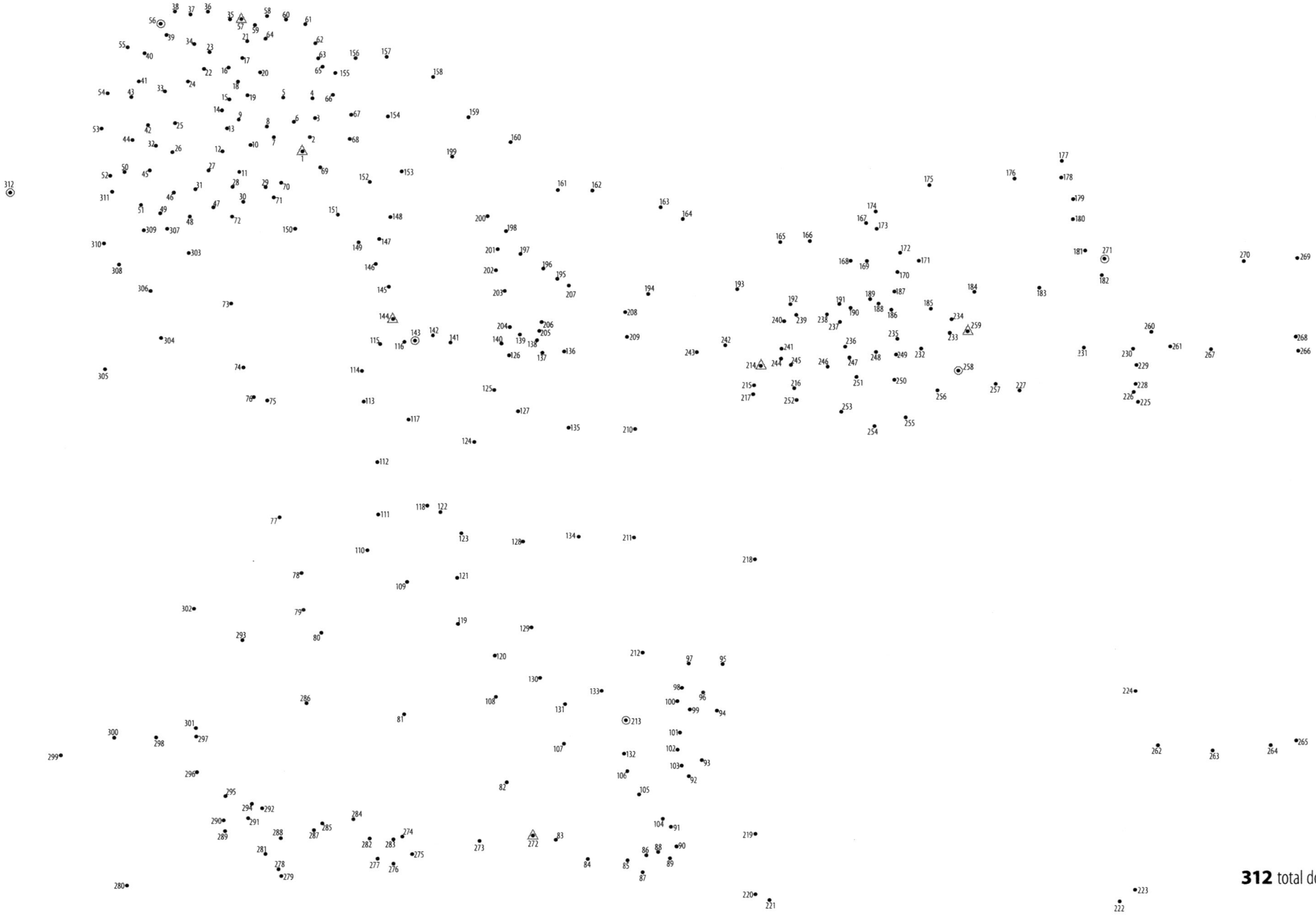

312 total dots

△ = Begin a new line section.

⊙ = Pick up your pen/pencil and look for the next sequential
number with the small triangle symbol next to it.

△ = Begin a new line section.

⊙ = Pick up your pen/pencil and look for the next sequential
number with the small triangle symbol next to it.

307 total dots

△ = Begin a new line section.

⊙ = Pick up your pen/pencil and look for the next sequential
number with the small triangle symbol next to it.

300 total dots

⚠ = Begin a new line section.

◉ = Pick up your pen/pencil and look for the next sequential
number with the small triangle symbol next to it.

356 total dots

⚠ = Begin a new line section.

⊙ = Pick up your pen/pencil and look for the next sequential
    number with the small triangle symbol next to it.

⚠ = Begin a new line section.

⊙ = Pick up your pen/pencil and look for the next sequential
number with the small triangle symbol next to it.

406 total dots

⚠ = Begin a new line section.

◉ = Pick up your pen/pencil and look for the next sequential
      number with the small triangle symbol next to it.

= Begin a new line section.

= Pick up your pen/pencil and look for the next sequential
number with the small triangle symbol next to it.

557 total dots

△ = Begin a new line section.

⊙ = Pick up your pen/pencil and look for the next sequential
number with the small triangle symbol next to it.

Plate 1 — *Mona Lisa,* Leonardo da Vinci

Plate 2 — *Girl with a Pearl Earring,*
Johannes Vermeer

Plate 3 — *The Scream,* Edvard Munch

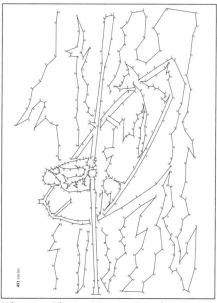

Plate 4 — *The Fog Warning,* Winslow Homer

Plate 5 — *Portrait of a Young Woman,*
Sandro Botticelli

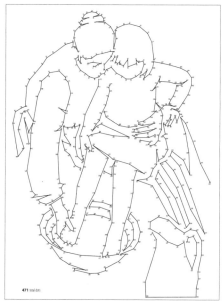

Plate 6 — *The Child's Bath,* Mary Cassatt

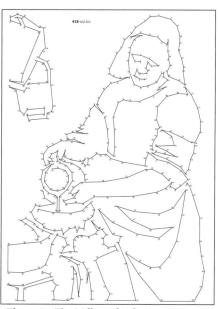

Plate 7 — *The Milkmaid,* Johannes Vermeer

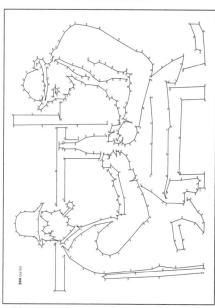

Plate 8 — *The Card Players,* Paul Cézanne

Plate 9 — *The Lady with an Ermine,*
Leonardo da Vinci

Plate 10 — *The Starry Night,*
Vincent van Gogh

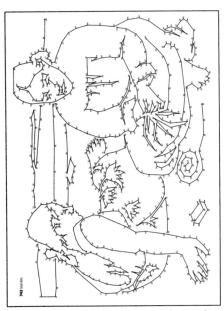

Plate 11 — *Tahitian Women on the Beach,*
Paul Gauguin

Plate 12 — *The Sleeping Gypsy,*
Henri Rousseau

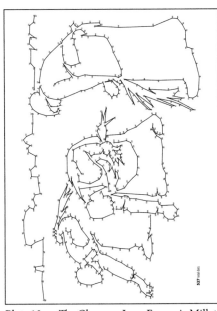

Plate 13 — *The Gleaners,* Jean-François Millet

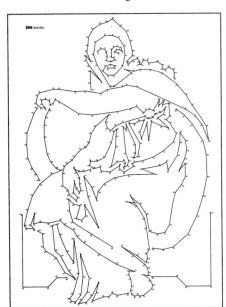

Plate 14 — *The Delphic Sibyl* (detail),
Sistine Chapel, Michelangelo

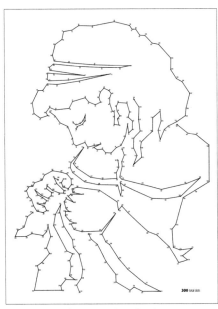

Plate 15 — *Lise Sewing,*
Pierre-Auguste Renoir

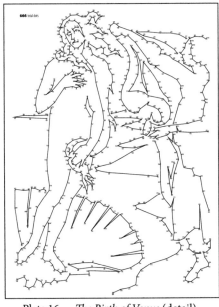

Plate 16 — *The Birth of Venus* (detail),
Sandro Botticelli

Plate 17 — *The School of Athens* (detail),
Raphael

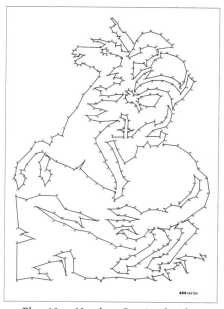

Plate 18 — *Napoleon Crossing the Alps,*
Jacques-Louis David

Plate 19 — *The Arnolfini Wedding,*
Jan van Eyck

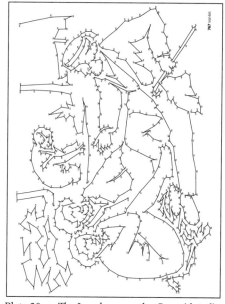

Plate 20 — *The Luncheon on the Grass* (detail),
Édouard Manet

Plate 21 — *A Warrior,* Rembrandt

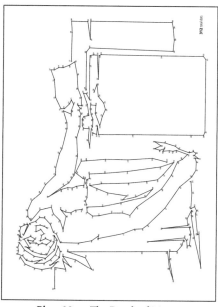

Plate 22 — *The Death of Marat,*
Jacques-Louis David

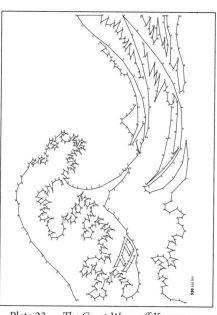

Plate 23 — *The Great Wave off Kanagawa,*
Hokusai

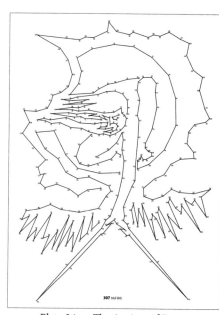

Plate 24 — *The Ancient of Days,*
William Blake

Plate 25 — *St. Francis in Meditation,*
Francisco de Zurbarán

Plate 26 — *The Jockey,*
Henri de Toulouse-Lautrec

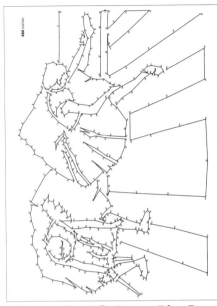

Plate 27 — *Two Ballet Dancers,* Edgar Degas

Plate 28 — *Self-Portrait with Bandaged Ear,*
Vincent van Gogh

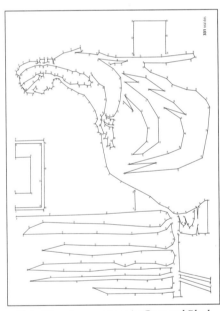

Plate 29 — *Arrangement in Grey and Black
No. 1 (Portrait of the Artist's Mother),*
James McNeill Whistler

Plate 30 — *Woman with a Parasol,*
Claude Monet